MW01644592

Sacred Alchemy

www.HealingWithLuLu.com

First Edition: October 2024

Published by Empower Healing LLC
Logo and page design by Hunab Amaya
Produced by Casey Higgins-Johnson

This book is dedicated to my mother, who walked beside me through it all when we both lost the most significant men in our lives: My grandfather and the love of her life, my father.

May you, too, find peace amidst unexplainable tragedy.

SACRED ALCHEMY

AN IMMERSION INTO THE SELF

An integrative process of viewing all of your life as sacred.

By Lindsay "LuLu" Simmons

Appreciation

The production of the book you now hold in your hands would simply not have been possible without two incredible women: Rebecca Schonebaum and Casey Higgins-Johnson.

Thank you, Rebecca, for helping to organize this masterpiece and disaster in its very early stages. It was alongside you that this book began to go from information overload to tasty, bite-sized morsels. Together we split the book into two, then into four, and then into eight. It was a labor-intensive process; it was the fiercest form of "unattachment" I have ever practiced, and it was entirely essential. Rebecca, your belief in me as a writer and the conversations we shared will stay with me forever — the tears, the chills, the laughter, and our big visions for our futures.

Casey, mi niña, mi amor, mi familia, I do not even know where to begin with you. In some ways, you've saved my life — like, the actual enjoyment of life — because before we met I didn't really have much of a life outside of my work. Casey is the woman behind the scenes over here. She is the Capricorn to my Cancer, the yang to my yin, and the person who helps me bring the medicine of my heart into this physical plane. She has my back and fiercely holds me steady. She is the partner in business that I prayed for, for years.

Casey, thank you for helping to birth my life's work into the world. This book would not physically exist without your love, your devotion, your belief in me, your eye for design, and the countless hours you spent editing. You made this real for me, sister. I love you more than words can say.

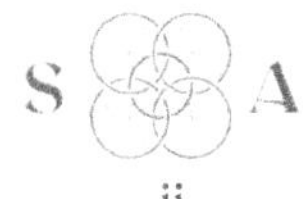

Contents

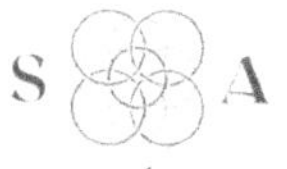

Preface

Have you ever felt like you *had* to make something? Like, you couldn't sleep until you made it? Couldn't return to normal? Couldn't move forward?

That is this book for me. I had to write it. It *had* to come through me. It had to be written by me, and writing it has changed my life while also showing me the purpose for all that I have gone through: The good, the bad, and the ugly.

You see, healing is my birthright; it's the whole reason I'm here. To heal myself, to heal my soul, to heal my lineage, to heal generationally and beyond. To benefit my family, the children I may give birth to one day, and any person I have the blessing of crossing paths with.

This book is a powerful alchemical tool. It is your permission slip to heal whatever, whenever, however, and wherever. It is your permission to grow beyond a healer and to become something even more true to your original essence.

To remember, perhaps, that there was never anything to heal because you were already whole — you just forgot who you were.

This book is a symbol of your empowerment: Your choice, your healing, your tenacity, your love, your journey, and your path, because you are meant to know your true nature.

This is a powerful reminder that there is always somewhere to begin. There is always something you can do to create positive change in your life. You just have to be willing to open to it.

My hope is that these words, tools, practices, and love notes bring you hope and remembrance. Hope to continue, hope to move forward, hope to heal, and hope for peace forevermore.

I also hope that you remember you are not ever alone, no matter how many times you journey to your own private island of suffering inside your mind, separating yourself from all that you are and all you can be. You are not now, and not ever, alone.

May this knowledge guide and nurture you at the deepest level, help you to feel supported and seen, and lead you inward to your true nature.

With love and gratitude,

Introduction:

Where it all began

This is the story that changed my life, and still is...

On May 12, 2008, my father died. I was 20 years old.

The world lost one of the best fathers, and with him, I lost myself. I lost LuLu, his girl. I lost the girl who never needed approval from any man. The girl who never doubted herself. A force to be reckoned with. Part of my heart went missing – and I desperately sought to fill that space with anyone or anything I could find. But nothing could ever fill me, and so I remained lost; lost to myself and to my place in the world.

For years I wandered in that emptiness, searching for pieces of myself in places I never belonged. I tried to be someone else, tried to be what others expected of me, and tried *anything* to ease that ache inside my soul that kept whispering, "He left me."

My father was *huge*. Not just big in my life, but physically huge. He was nearly seven feet tall with massive hands that looked like they could hold the whole world inside them. And having a phantom limb that size made me feel invisible. The more I searched to fill the void, the further I drifted from the person my father believed I could be: The person I was, so effortlessly, when he stood beside me.

Slowly, I began the journey back home to myself and to the girl who once stood tall in the shadow of her father's love. It wasn't easy. Every step felt like clawing pieces of myself back that had been ripped away from me. There was a permanent scowl on my face most days. Yet, somehow I had to learn how to stand on my own, without the safety of those giant, comforting hands that always held me steady.

| The Journey

The ten years following my father's death were filled with every single emotion. And many second and third helpings of the most painful ones.

I drank until I blacked out in year one. I abused sleeping pills because they took the pain away. I took antidepressants for over three years, tried different kinds of anti-anxiety meds for my panic attacks, and went on and off birth control in an attempt to regulate my hormones. I'd look in the mirror and see a dried up, hollow shell staring back at me, wishing me to look away from her once again.

I tried starving myself, imagining that skinny girls didn't have any problems. I binged, I purged, and then hated myself. In truth, I have hated myself and my body more times than I care to admit. I tried blaming everyone else for my struggles; I was selfish and angry and frustrated and pissed off at God for *years*. I also spent years being numb, nauseous, confused, sick, trapped, afraid, and broken. I asked, "Why me? Why him?" And: "What did I do to deserve this?"

On top of that, I harshly judged myself. For ALL OF IT. There was a soul-withering voice inside me critiquing every thought, word, and action I was taking, holding me to some version of *better* that was always too far off in the distance to achieve. Judgment is always the best icing on a shit cake.

And I'll tell you, one day I just decided that enough was enough. The next day I agreed. And the next, and the next. I was so sick and tired of feeling sick and tired. I knew there had to be *more* to life than this.

| The Choice

I decided to stop sitting in my own darkness. I decided to stop waiting for the answers to find me. I decided life is worth living and loving.

I remembered that between all of the pain and darkness, there were moments where I was happy. I laughed the same days that I cried, and while I may not have walked outside everyday, I looked out the window and dreamed with a hopeful heart of a life that was different.

I also remembered that *life is short*. My dad's death taught me that. Life is short, and precious. His death became my *why*. My point of no return. My, "I must get happy now, today, and everyday, because what else is there?" My father's death became my reason to live.

To get off all the drugs.
To get my body out of pain.
To get off the train to Negative Town.
To get out of crappy, emotionally abusive relationships.
To never, ever settle.
To find purpose. To find meaning.
To find LuLu.

One ordinary day that I cannot even remember, I chose myself. I followed my heart. I chose to live the life I was given. I decided what it was I actually wanted, and then I started creating it.

I decided to fight for LuLu; to fight for her (and sometimes with her) and to love her, every day, as he did.

This decision changed the course of my life.

It still breaks my heart that the best father a girl could ask for had to die in order for me to find myself. But I found her. I found LuLu all over again, and with her, I can do anything.

When I breathe now, I really breathe.
When I laugh now, I REALLY laugh.

When I sing, I dig deep into my heart and set her free like an uncaged bird. My heart is free to sing her song again and I can love more than ever before. When I dance, I feel a union. I can feel my own heartbeat in sync with my hips and the air around me.

I decided that my pain didn't have to be the end of my story. It could be my *catalyst*.

Today, I choose life. I choose to believe and see the best in people. I choose to believe that everything happens for a reason, and that sometimes things just happen — and I get to decide who and what I want to be in the face of both.

I choose to believe that every rejection is God's protection. I choose to take full responsibility for my thoughts, words, and actions. I choose to take action towards my dreams and learn through every experience, big and small.

I choose to believe that life is full of choices: To sink, to swim, to survive, or to thrive, but the choice is, and always was, mine.

And I hope you choose love.

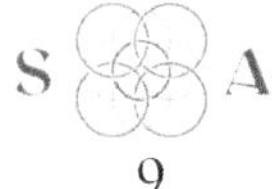

| Healing as an Unfinished Process

Healing is like learning; there are infinite things to discover, different aspects to explore, and new insights to open yourself to. To me, the healing process is an ongoing one. It's cyclical. So, just because I'm writing a book on healing doesn't mean I'm done healing – in fact, it's quite the opposite. This has been an illuminating, labor-intensive process full of patience, listening, and making space for the most current truth to reveal itself.

Every aspect of writing this book has been healing:

- Learning the tools, then putting them into practice
- Making up new tools when the original ones didn't work
- Re-writing the playbook over and over again
- Witnessing my clients use the tools to re-discover themselves, and learning through their eyes
- Discovering something new every time I work with someone

At first, the reason I studied and explored the information in this book so deeply was for myself. This is how I healed myself. And this is how I am still healing and opening myself to the infinite wisdom of my body, heart, and soul. I'm going to try and describe an example of this healing for you, so that you can recognize when it happens for yourself.

One night, after a full day of writing and two giant breakthroughs in the book, I laid down to go to sleep. I could still see the moonlight behind my closed eyelids when my root chakra* opened, spontaneously.

**A chakra is an energy center within the body. We dive deeper into this on page 46.*

It felt like a door opening at the base of my tailbone, and my whole being shifted. Just bam! It was a sensation I had never experienced before.

At the time, I had been living with tailbone pain for three solid years. The area ached, and sometimes nerve pain would spear through me from the bottom up. I had been desperately trying to move the energy there, silently inquiring with my body for months on end. Not-so-secretly hoping it would just *go away*, though I knew better than to hope for that. The body simply doesn't work that way with chronic pain. It's like expecting to win the lottery without buying a ticket.

While exploring my pain, I noticed that when I relaxed my perineum, the space anterior to the tailbone, my pain would decrease dramatically. My entire body would sing with relief and weightlessness. At the same time, I also felt embraced – somehow both free and held within my mind, body, and heart.

Relaxing my perineum was hard, especially at first. It was a delicate balance of surrendering and isolating certain muscle groups that weren't familiar to me. I had to open part of my body to relaxation and softness, while stabilizing another so that I still felt supported and safe.

So when I say that my root chakra spontaneously "opened", you also understand that it wasn't entirely spontaneous. It was a *breakthrough*. And somehow, the breakthrough I had while writing this book showed up as a breakthrough in my body.

I don't see myself as separate from the world around me. When things happen in my life, I can recognize that I created them and sometimes even why I needed to create them. And Opening energy channels as large as the chakras can be a very intense experience. At times, even euphoric.

Energy work in itself is quite euphoric, actually. When you work with energy, you are working with mystery: an unseen, etheric realm that is connected to the playground of the unknown. It's a godly realm often experienced through prayer when you truly surrender and rest in your faith.

You have a birthright to enter and explore this spiritual realm of creation and potential. You may never "know" what you're doing or feeling; like faith, you just trust and follow your heart. Experience, however, has taught me that following *that feeling* of lightness is an opening that often leads me to my desired destination. Following that feeling requires trust, and trust is gained through experiences of "following that feeling." I know, I know. I'm giggling here too. And I feel planted in this truth. It's just... true.

Here's my recipe for energy work:

- A little trial and error
- A little trust and surrender
- A little grace and remembrance
- And a great sense of humor

When my root chakra opened, I experienced the feeling of a weight lifting. It felt light, new, and curious, and it was an energy strong enough to make my body's protective mechanism activate and move away from the sensation.

I noticed this and coached my body to lean in more by deepening my breath, softening my body's protective grip, and choosing to explore with curiosity instead of moving away in fear.

This is a pleasure practice: Exploring sensation while creating safety through listening and nervous system regulation. When I did this, the energy opened more, and even more sensation poured through me.

I placed my hands on my belly and chest, reminding my body that we were in this together. I regulated my breathing, relaxed a bit more, and took my time until I felt the energy open up again – this time it moved inward, up my spine to the back of my heart.

"Whoa," I thought. "What the fuck is this?" Then I thought: "I don't care what it is. I want more." It felt good and was entirely self sourced. I continued to follow the energy's movements as it began to spread to the crown of my head, wrapping around me like the palm of a loving parent. I sipped in another breath, letting the warmth flow through me. Then I eased a breath out as the energy moved down my spine and up again, like a kind of dance back and forth.

"Am I being planted?" I thought. I also thought, again, "I want more."

This is a peek into how the body and mind speak to each other when you are the guide. To me, it's a practice of self-parenting and consent because both create the safety required for a truly holistic growth and healing process. I continued to follow the energy until my mind was so exhausted that my body went limp and I fell asleep. The next morning, I woke up with the same awareness and a fresh mind to explore with.

| You Are the Guide

The importance of sharing this “unfinished process” with you now is simple: You do not have to know what you’re doing in order to move forward in trust and with clear direction. *You are the guide.*

I had no idea what I was feeling and I had no lived experience to compare the sensation to. I do, however, have experience facilitating thousands of energy healing sessions. I have experience trusting and following the body’s intelligence, and I can stay with myself as I lean into a whisper or a sensation. And, I have enough wisdom to hold my own hand as I walk into the unknown.

This is healing. Just this. Staying true to yourself, trusting, and following your body’s intelligence. And holding your own hand. My best friend Jessica, who also happens to be one of the best coaches in the industry, has a mantra that I love:

“I don’t know. I don’t need to know.
And I will know what I need to know,
when I need to know it.”

Healing isn’t a task to complete or cross off your to-do list. In fact, your journey through the spiral of meeting yourself and your wounds will happen again and again in new ways, with new relationship dynamics, success, intimacy, etc.

That's the beauty of healing as an unfinished process. What we work on in our lives will continue showing up with new details and in new layers. If it didn't, we'd never see the progress we've made.

One more thing: Your wonderful mind wants to do everything it can possibly do to protect you. Your wonderful body wants the freedom to explore, create, expand, and play in the unknown. It is vital that the two learn to trust each other.

This trust is the foundation of an integrated healing process. It is a vital ingredient to building a healthy, dynamic relationship with yourself.

When you trust your body's wisdom and allow your mind to support (rather than control) the journey, you open the door to a whole new way of being. You stop fighting against the unknown and start moving with it, trusting that wherever you're headed, you are fully capable of guiding yourself there and giving yourself permission to enjoy the journey to becoming.

Healing isn't easy; embrace the process. Stay gentle with yourself, because the becoming is just as important as the being. Every wobbly step and uncomfortable moment is part of a greater unfolding, and an opportunity to know yourself more intimately.

Sacred Alchemy

A soul's journey to self healing

"Maybe the journey isn't so much about becoming anything. Maybe it's about un-becoming everything that isn't really you, so you can be who you were meant to be in the first place."

— Paul Coelho

This isn't just a book on self healing. It's a new set of keys; keys to unlocking the deeper pieces of who you truly are, and who you were always meant to be, before the world got ahold of you and told you what you cannot and could not ever be.

It's a doorway to imagination, wonder, possibility, and aliveness. It's a gateway to truth, unconditional love, and your original essence.

You are here to know yourself. And knowing yourself will reveal your soul's mission here. The journey is long and arduous and exactly what is needed for the magnitude of your inner evolution.

Your suffering is the doorway to your medicine.
Your heart is the courage to walk through the unknown.
Your soul is the lighthouse that is leading you home.

Are you ready to transform your suffering into medicine? Good. Then you are ready to become the alchemist of your own life.

You may be hearing a lot about alchemy these days, and not just from me. For that reason, I want to take this opportunity to define alchemy in my own terms and the terms that we will be exploring in this book series. To me, alchemy is a small part of a very forward way of thinking. I believe it's part of a new paradigm, a new foundation of philosophy we are collectively needing during these extraordinary and uncertain times.

Alchemy represents the medicine and transformation you crave. It's the shift in perspective you desire and it's the key to setting yourself free.

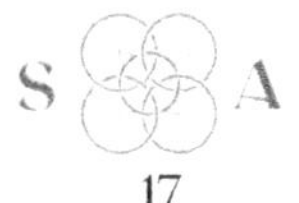

True transformation occurs within the shadows, the hidden aspects of yourself that you avoid and often deny love to. Your capacity to work with the shadow determines your capacity to hold the light. The world is currently in the fires of transmutation – a time of great alchemy of the soul, and you must become an alchemist.

The dictionary definition of alchemy is "a seemingly magical process of transformation, creation, or combination." To me, it's more about the process of creating something out of nothing; making lemonade out of lemons, so to speak. It's also a process of transforming fear into love, pain into fuel, and poison into medicine.

Transformation can mean taking two opposites and finding the common thread that links them. Transformation can mean holding multiple truths with neutrality and spaciousness. Transformation can also mean choosing to see hardship as a blessing and not a curse, letting it work with you and not against you.

Alchemy is a practice of truly claiming your sovereignty, autonomy, and authority over your own life: Past, present, and future. It's the illumination of the past brought through with a fresh perspective, the ability to transform your thoughts in the present moment, and the awareness you most desire following those beloved "ah ha" moments.

On a global scale, our lives have been massively disrupted and much is in chaos. I believe we are all being asked to alchemize our experiences right now. We are all being asked to "be the change" in our own lives, and this book is intended to be the "how to" of that philosophy.

It's easy to say the quote, and talk the talk, but what happens when it's time for action? Can you find the blessing in disruption, dismantling, and destruction? Can you embody the magnificent re-order that always follows chaos? How do you influence your own experience and become the living embodiment of the world you wish to create?

We are being asked to shift.
We are being asked to embody the truth of who we are.

Lead yourself from the unreal to the real,
from fear to love,
from shadow to truth,
from darkness to light.
Lead yourself to the home inside your bones,
and illuminate the truth of your being,
like a lotus flower grows,
unwaveringly through the darkest of shadows and
muck, toward the light, to bloom in its rightful
place: Glowing pristinely in the sun.

— My translation of an ancient Sanskrit prayer

Om Asato Maa Sad-Gamaya
Tamaso Maa Jyotir-Gamaya
Mrtyor-Maa Amrtam Gamaya
Om Shaantih Shaantih Shaantih

Alchemy & Embodiment

Living as who you truly are

When you are able to love yourself and your soul's journey wholly and completely, no matter what you have endured or suffered, then you have accessed the alchemical power of embodiment.

This is a book for your body. I hope the words on these pages support you in understanding the inner relationship you have with yourself and your body. To me, when you better understand your cognitive and psychological experience, it supports you in feeling safer in your body. You move from this feeling of uncertainty and separation to experiencing awe, wonderment, connection, understanding, and true, long-lasting safety.

Alchemizing your experience is a practice of becoming fully alive and present in your body and heart. Through practices like mindful movement, yoga asana, meditation (active rest), breathwork, and somatic expression, you practice dropping out of the logical, thinking mind and into the deep, innate wisdom of your body. Each time you bridge this gap between mind and body, you gain access to your true self, and you create new neural pathways in your brain.

The power of your true self lays dormant within you. And true enlightenment happens from the neck down. The power of your true self can easily transmute pain and trauma, release and integrate your emotions, and allow you to access your divine nature because you are love itself. It's the unconditional love and fire of devotion in your heart that allows true alchemy to occur.

Witnessing your body with this compassionate presence and acceptance is the foundation of embodied healing. Acceptance is the medicine of touching emotional wounds with deep, unwavering love. Through acceptance, alchemy occurs and your perspective begins to expand.

When your perspective begins to expand, you awaken to the unconditional freedom of being: Meaning your environment and external circumstances can no longer change your thoughts or behavior.

When you embody this deeper relationship with your true self, purpose, and desire, you are free to enjoy life in an elevated, expansive, and unconditional way. This freedom is the reason I wrote this book.

Take a deep breath and lean back. You are now holding a set of keys to open any door you may encounter. It's up to you which keys you pick up and which doors you choose to open. Use them wisely, and you'll find true and lasting freedom. You got this.

| Getting to Know the Language of Your Body

The body speaks in many different languages: Imagery, sensation, mood shifts, breathing changes, temperature, arousal, sound, and more.

When exploring a meaningful relationship, listening and curiosity are important. Remember what it's like to meet a new friend that you really vibe with or to spark a romantic connection with someone. You feel curious. You want to learn about them. You want to hear their story. You want to give them the benefit of the doubt.

The body works the same way; it wants to be in communication with you. It wants to know you're listening. It wants to respond and share its story, wisdom, and truth with you. It wants to know that you will believe it, even though you're not sure that what it's saying is true.

We live in a society with endless pull outward, towards media, towards others, towards expectation, towards obligation, and towards performance, all with a very fast-paced flow. We live in a culture that glorifies "doing" instead of "being." This external noise and rapid pace consistently agitates our bodies and scatters our energy and focus in many differing directions. All of this makes it challenging to hear the body's still, quiet voice.

So, to really listen and cultivate a relationship with your body's language, you don't just have to turn off your phone and pull your focus inward. You have to get comfortable with being yourself when there isn't something to produce or check off the to-do list. You have to learn to get quiet, to practice presence, to be alone with yourself, and to listen deeply.

Embodiment Play

How to drop out of the mind and into the body

Here's the part where the mind gets to rest. Ahhh, yes... no more thinking. Let your body lead the way now.

Try one or all of the following:

1. Take a deep breath into your lower belly, and a loud sigh out of your mouth (like a little kid would do.) Bonus points for sticking out your tongue and relaxing your jaw.

2. Dance in front of the mirror and make silly faces at yourself. You can have the devotion AND the humor.

3. Take your clothes off and walk around the house while listening to music. Feel the air on your bare skin.

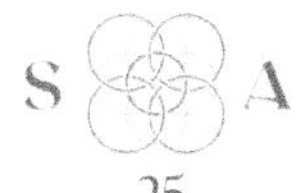

4. Look at your reflection and tell yourself how good you look today. Because hot damn, you do look good.

5. Pause and acknowledge how hard you're trying. You're not just trying, you're already taking action. Celebrate that.

| Simple Hands-On Listening Technique

Hands-on techniques influence the flow of energy in your body. This type of energy healing deepens your understanding of the tiny, endless changes that take place within your own body.

Sit or lay comfortably. Get cozy, close your eyes, and take a few deep, centering breaths. Connect to your body by placing your hands somewhere that feels sweet, easy, and nurturing. When your hands settle in, relax your elbows down and release your shoulders as well. Melt.

As you begin to relax, take a moment to greet yourself. Say "hello" in your own language. Listen for a response. It may help to listen with your heart. Just this simple act of greeting yourself the way you would greet anyone else is incredibly healing.

Smile. You just started a new relationship.

To go deeper, try asking your body a question such as: "*How are you? How are you feeling? What do you need most at this moment?*"

You may get a response in words or you may just feel exactly what it is: Hunger, sleepiness, agitation, etc.

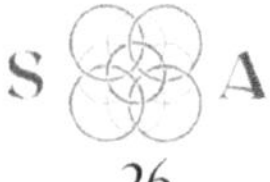

As my dear friend and former mentor Angie Byrd says, "*Questions are meant to be entered, not answered.*"

Enter the question with curiosity. Maybe you'll receive a clue. Maybe you'll receive an action step. Maybe you'll receive rest. Maybe you'll receive the inspiration of trying something new. Maybe you'll receive nothing. What you receive is perfect. If you want more, just keep inquiring.

To go even deeper, take immediate action on the answer you receive.

Taking action could look like drinking water, taking a five-minute nap, going for a walk, screaming, dancing, playing, wiggling, walking your dog, calling a friend, apologizing to yourself, crying, taking a bath, taking the day off, etc.

Take the action needed, and let the thoughts rest. When you take action on a message received from your body, you take a huge step forward into trust. The more action, the greater the trust and the louder and more confident your inner voice and intuition will become as a result.

MindBodyHeart

Where thought, feeling, and being become one

Mindbodyheart is a term I will use throughout this book series. It symbolizes everything I desire to create in *Sacred Alchemy*: Union, connection, and wholeness. Mindbodyheart is a tribute to the understanding that you and I are one holistic unit. Your mind is not disconnected from your heart; they were literally created in the same space, at the same time, in the same body. Though they have unique functions from one another, it is only social and societal conditioning that makes them appear separate.

Here's what each part represents to me:

- **Mind:** The masculine, stabilizing, structure-seeking element that is looking for stability, certainty, and sameness. The mind represents intelligence, something that is gained through the seeking of knowledge and the repetition of information and experiences. For the purposes of creating a new relationship and a bit more playfulness, we are going to refer to the mind as "he". It is also vital to the masculine mind that there be stimulation, systems, predictability, and safety, so that "he" can provide the support the body needs.

- **Body:** The feminine, changing, and ever-expansive element that is looking for more: More space, more love, more creativity, more satisfaction, and more beauty. It is the feminine nature to expand, spread out, and explore unknown territory. We are going to refer to the body as "she" in this new and playful relationship we are creating. It is vital to the body that there be silence, listening, nurturing, and safety so that "she" can continue to open to more beauty, creation, and magic.

- **Heart:** The union of opposites. The heart is the healer that can hold opposites ("he" and "she" and everything in between) and allows transformation to occur in a nourishing and loving way. The heart loves unconditionally; it doesn't care that the mind and body are opposites. It loves and supports both equally, and without hierarchy. While being in the body, the heart is also composed of neural cells from the brain's original creation in the womb, making it uniquely qualified to make decisions, support healing, and guide your path forward. The heart is where true alchemy exists, in the paradox where multiple truths can exist at the same time and are surrounded by love, patience, and unconditional support.

| Embodiment: The Somatic Experience

When you hear the word "somatic," what is your first thought? Maybe you remember that *soma* translates as "body" in Greek. Maybe you feel invited into the depth of your being and your breath because you remember a somatic healing session you had once. Maybe you feel curious to explore more because you've never heard this word before.

Somatic exploration is an inquiry with the deepest wisdom we have access to: The body. It's a remembrance and a union with the wholeness inside. Through the process of exploring the body's intuitive language, we begin to know ourselves with greater truth and accuracy. This truth of who we are allows us to navigate the constant and inevitable changes that occur around us. It is balance in its purest form.

In truth, we are living in an unprecedented world dynamic. Our body's nervous system is simply not designed to carry the stress that most of us navigate each day. Without understanding our mental health and the basic needs of our bodies, we can become disconnected, anxious, overwhelmed, and in a state of mere survival, fighting for our basic needs to be met.

One of the greatest challenges we face as a collective in today's post-pandemic world is fear. Fear of feeling, fear of connecting, fear of the future, fear of emotions, fear of death, and so on. Because of this, it's actually become a rarity to experience true safety: What it feels like to be completely safe with yourself. What is less rare is changing ourselves to meet the requirements of others.

In this ongoing search outside of ourselves for belonging and acceptance, we actually avoid our true feelings; the exploration of which would hold the most potent medicine we own. Instead, we actively abandon ourselves by refusing to feel our own feelings in order to meet our perceived needs of society and the world.

There's a term for this: **performative self abandonment.** I graciously thank whoever came up with this term because it so simply and adequately describes the greatest obstacle to true, authentic embodiment.

To me, performative self abandonment speaks to the fear we have of not belonging in the world, so we change ourselves to meet the requirements of belonging instead of exploring our own sense of belonging to ourselves... therefore losing touch with the most generous, intelligent, and holy aspects of who we are.

Somatic wisdom, the wisdom we hold in our bodies, is one of the most powerful ways we access our human potential. It's this wisdom that gives us the power to feel safe in every environment, express ourselves joyfully and freely in the world, and truly belong to ourselves. And a person who truly belongs to themselves thinks differently about everything.

Belonging is acceptance beyond superficiality.

The experience of physical and emotional belonging is the antidote for fear-based survival instincts. Belonging promotes an experience of relaxation and calm, while also inspiring confidence and positive self-esteem. When you're comfortable with yourself, you realize you belong everywhere.

This is an exploration into self-trust.

Together through this alchemical journey, we will explore a combination of both guided and unguided movement through open-ended questioning. Exploring, for example, who you become in the face of uncertainty and where you go (physically, mentally, emotionally) when you don't know what to do. Healing begins with awareness and a choice to change the storyline.

You gain a new perspective as you become aware of the filters you see your life through. When you can learn to be with yourself in the face of inner uncertainty, outer circumstances become less important because you know who you are, you trust who you are, and there's nothing that can truly change that but you.

This is a homecoming: Back to your body, breath, and innate wisdom.

A sacred journey begins with intention. Repeat out loud or in your own words:

For the duration of my healing journey, I devote my sacred power, precious focus, and priceless energy towards learning, honoring, respecting, encouraging, and awakening my own innate healing powers.

I have all that I need inside my mindbodyheart. I have all that I need inside myself. I now trust that the light of my soul is guiding me. I am taking time to honor and care for myself right here and right now, and will continue to do so throughout my self-healing journey here and beyond all space and time.

I ask that divine forces place their shield of love, truth, and protection around me now, permanently, so that only love and unlimited truth can exist between this book and me, between this journey and me. I thank you. I thank you. I thank you.

And so it is.

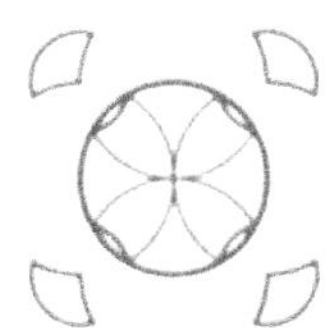

Energetic Influence

What you focus on is either fueling or depleting you

I should say from the beginning that I'm far from perfect. At my best, I give people the benefit of the doubt and make the most of everything that meets me on my path. At my worst, I make messes and I make mistakes. I pass judgements, I self-reflect, and then I make different choices.

Please consider my imperfections to be permission for you to also be an imperfect, soulful optimist. In fact, please be whatever you want to be. I love you like that.

It's important to note that all of what is written here was written by me, LuLu, and through the lens of my own experience. I, too, get overwhelmed by life during the growth process. So when I say I've been there, I honestly have. All of what I am choosing to share with you is embodied knowledge, which means I didn't read it in a book and regurgitate it here. I took knowledge from multiple trainings and various courses, brought the principles into my own life and private practice, got both curious and experimental, and spent years patiently piecing them all together. What I am sharing now is my own interpretation and the result of that curiosity and lived experience.

The lessons I've learned in my life have shown up in unexpected places, often when I'm far from any formal practice. They pop up out of nowhere when I'm traveling far from home, sitting in traffic trying not to lose my cool, or navigating a tough conversation. Life has a way of inviting us to apply what we know in the least predictable of ways, turning the ordinary moments into something profound.

And it's in those moments that I realized how true practice begins — not in perfect conditions, but in the messiness of life.

| Yoga Off the Mat

Yoga is not just a practice confined to a mat. In fact, it's in the real, raw moments of life that yoga truly reveals itself, when you get to see if your practice is actually working. The way we navigate our daily interactions, respond to challenges, and show up for ourselves and others is where the essence of yoga breathes. For me, this journey off the mat has been as much about learning how to be present with extreme discomfort as it has been about finding peace in stillness. This is how I took my yoga off the mat.

In my first CranioSacral Therapy training, I learned to practice "holds" along the body. As a class we were invited to place our hands on our client's body, holding them and listening deeply. We listened not with our ears, but with our hands and hearts. We placed one hand on the front of the body and one hand on the back, creating a sort of body sandwich, holding two sides of a chakra, diaphragm, or organ. This "hold" was intended to influence the movement of energy through their body. Through this gentle yet powerful technique, we invited the body's vital energy to move inward for the purpose of healing. We used our hands to signal the body to focus its attention, inviting its energy to gather itself in a specific area, rather than flowing outward.

This intentional redirection of energy is meant to amplify healing and boost the body's natural regenerative processes, while enhancing focus. When performed harmoniously, the client would enter a deeply relaxed, parasympathetic healing state, allowing the body's intelligence to take over. The results were often profound. What would happen was always different: Heat, pulsing, fluid movement, tingling, new blood flow, a deep breath, a yawn, a change in heart rate, or autonomic responses like eyelash flutters and body twitching (sometimes all at once). With each person I performed the technique on, I witnessed their body's wisdom reveal itself, showing me what it needed and how it needed it.

Much of what I understand about the body today comes from learning to interpret and translate this unspoken, somatic language and from these sessions of healing and communicating without words. Through this silent dialogue, I've come to see that the body holds its own wisdom, speaking volumes when we take the time to listen deeply. It was like talking to God every day; convening with the soul of the world and the soul of the individual at once. Maybe they're the same thing. To say it was extraordinary is an understatement; it was indescribable. It felt like meeting infinity.

These meetings with infinity taught me something profound: That healing, balance, and the wisdom of the body don't just happen in moments of stillness. They happen in every moment, simultaneously. This is where the true essence of yoga begins. Not just on the mat, but in how we choose to show up in life.

Yoga, or *union*, is applying that same deep listening and awareness to everyday experiences. It's a practice of recognizing the energy you bring into a conversation, the intention you carry as you walk through the world, and the way your body communicates with you when something feels right — or doesn't.

When you start to see life as yoga, you realize that the union of mind, body, and soul is happening everywhere. Every interaction, every step, every breath is an opportunity to tune into the wisdom that's always whispering to you in a language only you can understand. When you practice this kind of presence in everything you do, you allow the same deep healing and transformation that unfolds in those sacred, silent moments to weave through every aspect of your life, restoring neutral divinity in the gentlest and most harmonious way possible: Through the simple act of listening.

| Meeting the Soul of the World

When you truly understand energy, you realize how simple life is. Everything is energy.

Every thought you think, every word you speak, and every action you take carries energy. The fabric of reality itself — the air you breathe, the trees outside, your home, your body, and even this book — is all made of energy, vibrating and moving constantly. And within this vast, interconnected web of energy lies the key to healing.

What if I told you that healing is as simple as knowing how to move energy? That the body's natural state is one of balance, and with the right intention, focus, and gentle guidance, you can restore that balance? This isn't about controlling or forcing, it's about inviting your energy to shift, to flow, to return to wholeness.

This is what I'm hoping to teach you: How to influence the movement of energy to bring harmony back to your body, mind, and spirit.

So, how do you influence the movement of energy?

"I Cause"

The power of influence

| Mind

Energy is influenced in the mind through decision: Decisive intention, a shift in perspective, a mantra, and similar conscious choices. The mind represents the psychological aspect of this work, and it operates with the understanding that "*I am the cause of my effect. I create my own experience of reality.*"

When you make a decision, when you truly make up your mind, there is a unique and direct energetic signature that is created. This signature influences your actions, making it easier to take action and attain the result you desire. The mind is powerful. Each decision directly influences the body and heart. Through this exploration, you begin to see how your life shows up in your body.

Think about it: Your mind affects your heart. The heart may express a desire for love, tenderness, or support, but then the mind steps in, telling you that either you don't deserve it or aren't allowed to have it, with a long list of reasons why. You may even feel compelled to change who you are to receive love.

For example:

- I need to lose 10 pounds *to be loved*
- I need to finish that home project *to be worthy of rest*
- I need to be better looking *to be accepted*
- I need to have more money (or appear to) *to be valued*
- I need to change/be different than I am *to be worthy of love*

| Body

Energy is influenced in the body in three main ways:

1. Through the mind (decision)
2. Through physical movement (moving the body, manipulating the breath, physical cleansing, etc.)
3. Through the elements (food, water, minerals, plants, fire, air, ether, earth)

Your body mirrors what is occurring for you mentally and emotionally. It shows you the way your thoughts, beliefs, wounds, and desires affect you by translating them into physical sensations, postures, and health. To create lasting change in the body, you must influence not only your physical habits but also your mental and emotional landscapes.

Regulating your nervous system and shifting your emotional responses to external stimuli are key to this process. The body is more than just flesh and bone; it's a map of your internal world. It's a living computer that stores your feelings, thoughts, actions, and life experiences. It holds the memory of everything you've been through. In this way, your body is a mere reflection of your mind.

To truly understand and honor the relationship you have with your body, you must first understand how you think and feel. When you do, you'll see that your body is a mirror, showing you exactly where healing or alignment is needed.

For example:

- Shoulder tightness from bearing the weight of responsibility
- Neck tension from not feeling emotionally supported
- Shallow breathing when feeling anxious or overwhelmed
- Digestive issues when unable to process emotions or stress
- Fatigue from overextending and not honoring boundaries
- Tension in the jaw from suppressing anger or unspoken words
- A heavy chest when experiencing grief or sadness
- Lower back pain when feeling unsupported or burdened by life's demands

| Heart

Energy is influenced in the heart through alchemy. The heart is a powerful, medicinal tool; the way you think and the way you feel directly shape your physical experience. The emotional state you reside in influences your behavior, which in turn impacts your life.

As an alchemist, you agree to reclaim the creation of your life. You live as though you are the cause, not just the effect.

It's far more empowering to believe that you are part of the recipe rather than believing that things simply happen to you. As an alchemist, you recognize that everything, whether by coincidence or intention, can either contribute to your evolution or your destruction. And you get to choose which one it is.

The heart's high-frequency energy has the ability to heal both the mind and body. This is why, when people find spiritual devotion — whether through God, religion, or a deep inner connection — their entire life transforms.

Their life changes because their heart is changing, and the heart changes when beliefs and ways of thinking begin to shift. It's an ongoing alchemical process of awakening and coming alive.

By learning to influence energy, you free up energetic channels, allowing life to flow more easily through your body and mind.

For example:

- Choosing to view a difficult breakup as a catalyst for self-love and growth
- Shifting from a mindset of scarcity to one of abundance, allowing the heart to open to possibilities instead of dwelling in fear
- Allowing grief to become a pathway to deeper compassion and intimacy, transmuting the pain into connection with others

Examples, continued:

- Releasing the need for external validation, which transforms feelings of inadequacy into a sense of inner worth and confidence
- Turning anger into fuel for creating change, shifting the energy of resentment into empowerment and action
- Choosing forgiveness and transforming bitterness into freedom
- Viewing life's challenges as opportunities for evolution, transforming frustration or defeat into resilience and inner strength

We'll dive deeper into how the mind, body, and heart interact, how your thoughts shape your reality, and how healing your body can ultimately heal your life in the coming chapters.

The Inspiration Behind It All

"Religion is like holding on to a rock in the middle of a raging river; faith is learning how to swim."

- Unknown

Each chapter of this book is inspired by energetic anatomy. It's through this lens that we can explore some of life's more profound questions, like: "*Who am I? What is my true nature? What is the essence of my soul? Where am I limiting my potential? And what is truly possible?*"

Exploring energy invites you inward, discovering and rediscovering your subtle landscape and the intentions behind everything that occurs within and around you. It offers you perspective beyond the surface, allowing you to see the patterns that repeat in your life and the deeper truths they reveal. Through energetic anatomy, you gain insight into not just who you are, but who you have the potential to become.

The knowledge shared in this book is a blend of ancient wisdom, modern psychology, and the growing field of energy medicine.

At its core, the *Sacred Alchemy* book series is grounded in the *chakra* (CHAH-krah) system, which has been a guiding force in my own healing journey and what I worked with as a somatic healer and yoga teacher. My studies in traditional and yogic psychology, along with my experiences with clients, have all contributed to the wisdom woven throughout these pages.

So what exactly is a chakra, you might be wondering?

The most direct translation of the Sanskrit word chakra is "wheel." You can imagine it now as a spinning wheel of radiant light inside you, shifting and renewing your energy as you read these words.

This "wheel" moves in harmony with the rhythm of your life, directing and influencing your experience on every level – physically, emotionally, and spiritually.

Through the stories, teachings, and practices found in this book, you will embark on your own journey of awakening, peeling back the layers of your energy, beliefs, and limitations to reveal the alchemist within. And much like the quote about the river and the swimmer at the beginning of this chapter, this process is not about clinging to certainty. It's about learning to flow with the currents of life.

| Energetic Anatomy: Understanding the Subtle Body

Your human body is made of energy. You are flesh and bone, of course, and you are also composed of the most subtle aspects — from atoms and neurons to energetic layers of perception. It is within these aspects that your **subtle body** exists, influencing your physical body in profound and often unseen ways.

Through the study of ancient Vedic and Yogic philosophy, we now know that our body is composed of energetic channels called *nadis* (NAH-dees). Nadis are tube-like channels that form a vast network, moving prana, or life-force energy, throughout your human body. *Prana* (PRAH-nah) is the very essence that animates you. It moves through your body and also expands outside your body through the ancient Chinese meridian system, which accompanies the nadis. Where the nadis, meridians, and the systems they comprise merge is within the spinal cord — our body's command center, and what many yogis call the "central channel."

You may already know that the brain and spinal cord make up your body's nervous system. What you may not know is that your nervous system also acts as part of your **energy body**, guiding how you respond to every experience in your life. In order to understand how the nervous system impacts human psychology and somatic experience, I feel it's important to understand the basics of how your energy body functions.

Nadis and chakras at lower, more foundational areas in the body vibrate at lower frequencies and are connected to more primal, physical concerns, such as survival instincts and your sense of identity in the world.

Based on Vedic philosophy, there are three primary energy channels, or nadis, within the human body:

- **Ida (EE-dah) Nadi** resides on the left side of your body and represents your feminine, yin element. It is connected to your inner waters and internal experience, often reflecting how you treat yourself. If you find it difficult to receive support, struggle with being still, or have trouble listening to your inner voice, you may be experiencing an imbalance in the ida channel.

- **Pingala (PIN-gah-lah) Nadi** resides on the right side of your body and represents your masculine, yang element. It governs your inner fire and external experience, mirroring how you interact with and support others. If you struggle with offering help or support to others, or feel uneasy completing physical tasks, this may indicate an imbalance in the pingala channel.

- **Sushumna (SOO-shoom-nah) Nadi** runs through the central spinal column and represents your spiritual awareness, higher self-knowledge, and self-actualization. This central channel is amplified and purified through acts of kindness toward yourself and others. Difficulty with kindness, feeling disconnected from subtle energies, or struggling to connect with the divine may signal an imbalance in the sushumna channel.

In Vedic philosophy, it is believed that when these nadis are clear and your chakras are spinning freely, you experience a state of total bliss: A yoga, or union, with the divine source of all creation.

In Western society, these blissful states are more commonly experienced in moments, hours, or occasionally days. Prolonged states of union are less common and require dedicated practice, self-actualization, or an intentional and curated environment to sustain.

The nadis travel throughout the body and spinal column, constantly intersecting each other. When all three nadis intersect, a powerful energetic vortex is created. This vortex is what Vedic philosophy refers to as a chakra. It's an energetic command center and a union of the left channel (ida), the right channel (pingala), and the central channel (sushumna).

The most notable chakras merge at seven distinct junctures along the central channel or spine. Each chakra is envisioned as the shape of a wheel, sphere, or globe. These energy centers fill space within the body and radiate energy outward, beyond the physical form. Chakras can also be called "gates of perception" because of their profound ability to influence your physical reality and how you, then, perceive the world around you.

There is an entire world of complex systems at play in the subtle bodies of our physical form. Each of the seven primary energy centers, and the somatic and psychological principles they inspire, will be explored in-depth throughout the *Sacred Alchemy* book series. While we'll explore each topic individually, it's important to remember that, just like you, they are all part of one complete and interconnected system. We study the part to understand the whole. Any shift in one area of your body impacts your entire system, which ultimately affects how you experience life.

When Wayne Dyer said, "If you change the way you look at things, the things you look at change," he was speaking about the power of your perception. Nothing in your life needs to shift on the outside for everything to change on the inside.

Your relationship with everything can completely transform within your mindbodyheart without anything shifting in your external environment.

This journey is an in-depth exploration of how your life shows up in your body and how your external reality reflects your internal state. Together, we will explore how shifting your internal landscape can change your relationship with everything, revealing that healing is truly an inside job.

Sacred Alchemy is a roadmap, connecting dots in your life that initially seem unrelated while strengthening your relationship with the most powerful instrument you own: Your body. We will journey through foundational and subtle aspects, exploring the house that your soul calls home and providing you with new keys to unlock common obstacles in life.

As we explore the intricate relationship between energy and the body, it's important to remember that healing happens on multiple levels. While the physical body is powerful, the energy and emotional bodies play an essential role in the healing process.

This became especially clear to me when I started experiencing teeth-clenching pain in my lower back and neck. It was during this time that I realized true transformation requires honoring both the subtle and the physical aspects of ourselves. What I was learning about energy needed to be integrated into my physical body as well...

| Everything Is Energy

In 2012, the pain in my neck and lower back was so sharp, so pervasive, that I started grinding my teeth during the day. It scattered itself up my spine and down my legs as I bent over my massage table. It was the kind of pain that grips you tightly, sinking its claws in, refusing to let go. I don't think I breathed deeply that whole year, only taking in shallow sips, hoping not to awaken the beast beneath the pain. My body, once a being of movement and ease, felt like it was turning against me.

In early January of that year, I pushed my body beyond its limits while practicing a new style of yoga that I had found after a heart-wrenching breakup with a soulmate (more on that later). I had been forcing myself repeatedly into a deep backbend called "wheel pose," unwisely trying to push myself upward with the back of my head. In doing so, I sprained my neck. The pain was so excruciating, so sharp and searing, that I was put in a neck brace. I could barely drive my car, and even the tiniest bump or turn would send shockwaves of pain through my entire body. I would swallow hard, trying not to make it worse, but it felt as if every part of me was on high alert, screaming with each movement.

I probably would have cried more if I hadn't been so locked up emotionally. The pain wasn't just physical, and I could really feel it. My body was holding onto everything; the grief and heartbreak of that loss, the tension of forcing myself to keep moving forward. All of it zipped up inside, clamped down as tightly as my muscles.

I learned more about my unique flavor of neck pain during yoga teacher training later that summer, when my neck spontaneously sprained again.

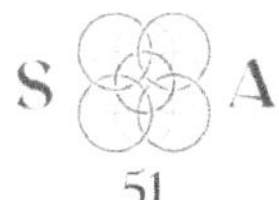

This time, the pain suspiciously seared down the left side, the opposite side of my neck from the January injury. I knew then — I *just knew* — there was something more to this pain.

My teachers kept asking me what I did, and each time I said "nothing," I received the same raised eyebrows and pursed lips until I followed up with, "It's not physical." Their faces softened at that, in silent understanding. For me, it was validation of what I had intuitively known all along: This pain was the quiet scream of an emotion, simmering just below the surface, *waking up*.

That injury only compounded in the fall of that year when I began receiving sharp, probing pulses of pain in my lower back. The intense and constant pain I had been feeling in my neck had eased into a dull, ever-present ache, just in time for my lower back to start screaming in September.

But as you may already know, physical pain pales in comparison to emotional pain. I endured months of physical suffering because I wasn't ready to face what was hiding beneath it — the emotions I had neatly stored there, slowly strangling the light within me.

At the time, I was 25 and supporting myself financially as an independent contractor and entrepreneur. I worked as a massage therapist at three different businesses while selling MLM (multi-level marketing) products on the side. Every day I'd brace myself for the pain, holding my breath and pushing through it as I leaned into the massage table during my treatments.

I would clamp down, forcing my body to cooperate as waves of tension hit me from all sides.

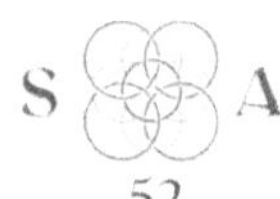

The urge to buckle over and collapse onto my clients was ever-present, but I endured, unsure if there was a way to work without it. I hid the pain and kept it to myself because I was afraid that if I told anyone, they wouldn't let me work. And as a single 25-year-old with school debt and very adult responsibilities, I knew that if I didn't work, I couldn't live.

Early the following year, I moved in with my dear friend, Saramel. She'd seen me wincing in pain around the house and modifying my yoga practice so that I could move with less agony during the sequences. It didn't take her long to give me the number of her chiropractor, a man she's rewarded with many adoring titles — including, but not limited to, "the man who saved her life."

I had his number stored in my phone for months and never looked at it. It was the same old story: I was too stubborn, too busy, and too overwhelmed to reach out for help. And, honestly, I didn't believe it was going to work for me. Most chiropractors, in my experience, were like bad car salesmen. The ick was real.

One day I could barely turn my head, and the pain radiated like fire down my spine. As I sat on the couch wincing, Saramel stormed over, lifted my phone from the ottoman, and dialed his number before handing it back to me. She knew I needed a nudge. And, surprise surprise, that call changed everything. I still see him to this day, and he's the most gifted and devoted doctor of chiropractic I've ever met.

You might be thinking, "*LuLu, chiropractic is physical work. What does this have to do with energy?*"

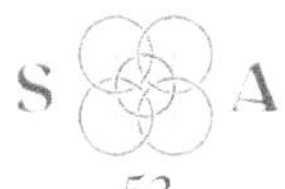

Let me explain.

Chiropractic care works directly with the nervous system — the energetic command center of the body. When your nervous system is compromised, everything is affected. The flow of energy is disrupted, and your physical, emotional, and mental states are thrown off balance.

If the vertebral column is subluxated, or severely misaligned, you can experience nausea, vomiting, or diarrhea, feel depressed, and have a long list of strange symptoms that appear unrelated.

Here's the paradox: While I was focusing on healing my energy, releasing old patterns and emotional wounds, I had neglected the physical body that housed it all. I learned then that you must care for both the energetic and the physical bodies *simultaneously* if you are to truly heal.

During this painful chapter of my life, I realized that in order to move through the experience and come out on the other side, I needed to honor my body in a new way. The reason I can now sit here pain-free, writing these words, is because I was doing this alchemical work — mind, body, and spirit.

The chiropractic care worked because the energetic medicine I was practicing allowed it to. Because I was seeing my pain as a symptom and not a problem, I was choosing my holistic health. This is where true healing occurs. Physical medicine alone cannot reach the deepest layers unless energetic shifts are happening too. Physical medicine works when alchemical medicine works; they are meant to harmonize with each other.

Long-lasting relief occurs when foundational shifts happen in both mindset and behavior. To only address one is to address merely one part of a whole system. The chiropractic adjustments worked for me because my body was open to receiving the healing, and the medicine could actually get in. It became more than manipulation of bones and joints — it became a holistic, transformative process. When psychosomatic healing meets physical medicine, the results are powerful, integrated, and lasting.

Here's the truth: When it comes to healing, the physical body is the last to shift. Emotional and energetic shifts must occur in order to experience physical relief.

Chronic pain doesn't just disappear on its own — it unravels as you begin to address the patterns of dysfunction that exist at the root. Only then can chronic pain begin to disperse, dissolve, and disappear. When you can release the energy of past trauma, unresolved emotions, and harmful belief systems, you pull the root of the pain out, allowing your physical body to finally release the suffering.

You are a whole being, and healing is a holistic process. Alchemy embraces every aspect of who you are — physical, emotional, mental, and spiritual. Although the physical body may be the last to reflect these changes, there are countless unseen victories happening throughout your journey. Each subtle shift is building the foundation for deep, lasting transformation.

As humans, we often feel more connected to the physical. Pain demands our attention.

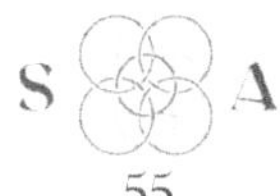

But I encourage you to go deeper — to make contact with the subtle body that lies beneath the surface, shimmering with information.

The more you bring awareness to this subtle layer, the more harmony you begin to create between your physical and energetic bodies. This is where real healing happens.

| Emotion Is Energy

Emotions are how energy expresses itself in the body and are often referred to as "energy-in-motion." Emotions move through you, influencing your physical experience in profound and invisible ways.

When emotions aren't fully processed or expressed, they can become trapped, creating tension, discomfort, or even pain in the body. They may slowly poison your present-day experiences with your unhealed past. These physical reactions are your body's way of channeling the emotional energy.

This concept of emotions as "energy-in-motion" helps us understand how powerful and interconnected the emotional and physical bodies are. When we start to notice how our emotions manifest physically, we open the door to deeper self-awareness and healing. This idea was illustrated beautifully by one of my teachers in massage school.

My teacher, Patrick, had a long-time massage therapy client who struggled with fibromyalgia. He worked with her tirelessly, lost with her at times in the confusion surrounding this disorder. Fibromyalgia, or fibrosis, is commonly associated with widespread pain and tenderness in the muscle tissue. It affects the body physically through pain, emotionally through mood swings and depression, mentally through memory loss, and energetically through chronic fatigue and exhaustion. At the time, there was said to be no cure for this disorder, and Patrick thought that was bullshit.

During his years of house calls, Patrick watched his client suffer without relief. He talked with her, tried physical massage and energy healing techniques, and gave her tips that she usually didn't implement because, well, suffering creates little motivation when you're attached to it.

Patrick believed fibromyalgia is, at its core, a psychological and psychosomatic dis-order. He felt that, while the pain manifested physically, the root cause seemed to stem from something deeper; something buried in the emotional and psychological layers of his client's life. He believed her pain was a reflection of her extraordinary unhappiness and the heavy burdens she carried. Burdens that had become heavier each year she carried them.

It wasn't just the pain in her muscles. He felt the emotional weight that had been stored in her body over time manifesting as chronic pain and exhaustion. The disorder, as Patrick saw it, was a mirror to her inner turmoil, a signal from her body that something needed to be addressed. He knew that true healing would require unearthing the emotional wounds that had been suffocating her vitality for years.

Then, one day, everything changed. Patrick arrived for a session expecting the usual style and flow, but when his client opened the door, she was smiling. The heaviness that had clung to her seemed lighter, as if it had lifted. She looked at him with a brightness he had never seen before. When she told him she was experiencing very little pain, Patrick was instantly curious. He had to know what had shifted so drastically. He asked her what had changed, eager to understand what had caused this sudden improvement.

Her answer was simple, but powerful: "I fell in love."

She had met someone new, and as they spent time together, the feelings of love and connection began to fill the spaces where pain had once resided.

As her emotional landscape shifted, her pain faded. The joy and affection she was experiencing seemed to be healing her in ways that physical medicine alone could not. As she fell in love, her body responded; it was as though her muscles and tissues were finally letting go of years of held tension, dissolving in the wake of hope, love, and companionship.

Patrick watched as her body, no longer trapped by pain, began to move with ease again. The love she felt wasn't just emotional — it was healing her and allowing her body to open to something new.

For me, hearing this story was a lightbulb moment. It was the first time I truly understood how much the emotional body impacts the way we experience ourselves, our bodies, and our lives. I also felt really *seen*. I knew I was meant to be right there, in that classroom, listening to that story and awakening to an ancient remembrance within me.

I realized then that healing isn't just about addressing physical symptoms. There is really something to exploring the emotions beneath them. Since then, I've learned and experienced that emotions are powerful. When we allow ourselves to feel them fully, we create space for profound healing, both inside and out.

Reflections

Making sense of what shows up in your life

Take a deep breath in. Open your mouth and let it fall out with a sigh.

Invite yourself into a sacred pause.

If it feels good, close your eyes and let the stories you just read wash over you, allowing them to filter through your being like water through a drip coffeemaker.

Take this moment to breathe and connect: Be with your body, return to your intention, and release logic for a while. Welcome your intuitive intelligence to step forward.

How do you feel about what you just read?

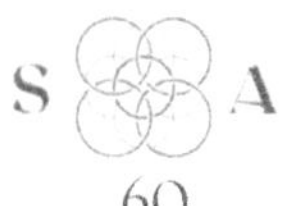

Feel free to take this opportunity to light a candle, put on some music, take out your journal, and allow yourself to open by writing down what is coming up for you so far. Silently ask yourself:

What stands out to me?
What "Ah Ha" moments are coming into view?
What am I seeing differently?
What do I feel resistance around?

Write linearly, or write in a stream of consciousness. Trust yourself and what comes through you. Do not try to control it. Let it flow. Keep the channel open.

Sometimes when we're doing this work, we get so deep into it that we relate everything to it... and sometimes, things just happen.

Remember to lighten up. You do not have to digest and understand everything. You do not have to agree with me, ever. The invitation here is to inquire within and decide for yourself: "*What's true for me?*"

In healing work, zooming out is just as important as zooming in. Regardless of where you go from here, go with yourself and with a sacred intention. This is your life, and you get to decide how you meet it.

| The Feather, the Brick, and the Semi

First and foremost, I cannot take credit for this witty analogy. I've heard it said in many different ways and by many different people. I didn't come up with the terms, but I can easily describe and relate to exactly what they mean. Maybe you can, too.

Intuitive messages, or what some may call messages from the Universe/God, come to us in different ways. Almost always they begin with a whisper. You get a feather-light nudge; it's so soft and sweet, you almost don't notice it at all. When you do notice it, you may dismiss it. I mean, it's so subtle, it can't really be true... right?

Ah, so maybe you ignore this message and let life go on as usual. It whispers to you from the back of your mind, but it's only a feather. Maybe this feather is an intuitive hit to start something that could be prosperous. Maybe it's a nudge to enter a new relationship. Maybe it's your body saying it doesn't like something. And maybe it's the whisper of a long-denied truth about yourself or another.

The feather seems almost unnoticeable... yet it's strong and potent like the truth always is. Small enough to ignore and big enough for you to know it's coming back, for certain. But that's in the future, and we don't have to worry about that right now, right? I hope you're smiling as you catch on to the foreshadowing here.

Then, one fine day, the feather returns... but this time, it's a brick.

A solid brick that can feel like a punch and leave a mark. The feather was so sweet and soft; the brick is hard, direct, and unforgiving. It knocks you over the head when you're least expecting it.

When the brick comes in, its voice is not quiet. The brick gives a push to stop procrastinating. You trip over and fall into the thing you've been avoiding, some kind of health issue pops up in your body that is difficult to ignore (ouch), and that truth you've been denying or the relationship you were supposed to leave is feeling like it's on fire. All of a sudden, that little feather is feeling like a kick in the ass, and you're looking for a solution ASAP.

The brick is very uncomfortable, but hear me when I say that it's not as loud as it gets. You'd be surprised by just how many bricks a person can tolerate. So maybe you grin and bear it. Maybe you put off *that thing* a little longer, hoping it will pass or just resolve itself. Right?

This is the part where the message gets big. Like, semi truck big. But first...

I've noticed in my own life that there can be another level between the brick and the semi. Maybe it's "the boulder," or a tree that literally falls on your house one day out of the blue. (This actually happened to a student of mine during a yin yoga class.) My point is, there is a big difference between the brick and the semi.

When the Universe throws you a brick, you may feel very uncomfortable — but not uncomfortable enough to change anything.

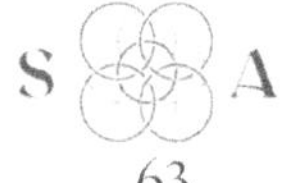

Then the boulder comes in and you start to slowly (or quickly) change things, and your messages from the Universe move back down to brick and feather sizes. Hopefully.

A message from the Universe the size of a semi truck is life altering.

The semi presents as a life experience like a car crash, a health crisis, a non-fatal accident, a death in the family, or something big enough to give you a very loud, megaphone-style message. This kind of message shakes you, sometimes to the core of your being, and makes you rethink decisions you've been making or have made in life.

It can quite literally knock the wind out of you. There's nothing subtle about it.

The semi often represents what you might call a rock bottom moment, or a wake-up call that you can't ignore. And sometimes, it can be what I call *the point of no return.* Something happens in your life that leaves more than just a scar and wakes you up to a whole new experience that you can never truly "un-wake up" from. You cannot un-know what you know after the semi.

While these moments are powerful teachers, I've learned that there's wisdom in not waiting for life to reach that point. Over time, I've made an agreement with myself to tune into the smaller messages; the whispers and the feathers.

I realized that I don't have to wait for the bricks and boulders to crash into me.

Instead, I can learn from love; I can be initiated by love. I can tune into the subtle nudges that life sends my way, allowing for gentler lessons and smoother transitions.

When the semi does show up, however, you can courageously choose for it to be the best thing that ever happened to you. You can let it be the reason you make your dreams come true, or the encouragement you need to find true and lasting happiness without the guilt.

You may have to fight for your life, but the passion you'll have for your life following that fight is something money cannot buy. It's a kind of transformation that alters the way you experience everything.

But again, you don't have to wait for that level of intensity. You can receive the messages and lessons you need without life hitting you where it hurts.

When you start looking at signs and symbols you receive from your body and the Universe, it may help to think of them in terms of their metaphorical, or literal, size. When you have a new perspective on how your body and life communicate to you, it may support you in choosing more wisely.

Maybe you've been waiting for the bricks and boulders to fall, thinking that change only comes when life forces you into it. But it doesn't have to be that way. You can listen to the whispers, choosing to stop forcing, controlling, or resisting what is meant for you. These subtle nudges can guide you before the lessons get harder.

Imagine making an agreement with yourself to follow the whispers and the feathers, to learn loving lessons that are gentle in their power. The choice to listen early is an act of self-love and an invitation to engage with life in a way that honors your wellbeing.

Reflect on times when you received a feather, a brick, or even a semi. How did you respond, and what did you learn? If it feels supportive, grab your journal and ask yourself: "*Where am I being nudged by a feather, and how can I follow its guidance before the message grows louder?*"

The other important piece to note is that sometimes, things really do just happen. I believe that! Not everything is a powerful message from the cosmos. Sometimes a shoe is just a shoe... not a sign to call a past lover and start again.

And, when you're on the spiritual path, everything in your experience can assist your evolution and alchemy if you are open to it. (Even the shoe that's just a shoe.)

Common Obstacles

Meeting “La Résistance”

The speed at which you learn is often tied to how much resistance you feel towards what you’re learning.

As alchemists, we dive into intensity in order to understand our power. Part of our journey is testing the limits to our own capacity. Through that process, we get to discover each day where our edges are and gently lean into them. We see where we can feel big things and do hard things and thrive inside of them, not in spite of them.

No part of your past has to rule you.

Let’s talk a little about resistance. And, if it feels right, invite your sense of humor to join us here. Whether you like it or not, your resistance (and hopefully your sense of humor and compassion) is going to be your dance partner on this healing journey.

A little humor, a lot of compassion, and yes, plenty of resistance. That's usually how it goes. It's okay to feel it all, and it's okay to invite it all in. Better to make friends with your resistance than to continue the inner war, right? You're on the same team, after all.

Resistance is a powerful force. But remember, it's here to protect you. It's not your enemy; it's on your side. I invite you to greet it now with a spacious breath and an open heart. Allow your resistance to join this process with you as your partner, not as an obstacle.

Take a moment to acknowledge that there is a part of you that may not want to grow, heal, or change. This part wants to stay in the familiar. And that's okay. It wants to stay the same, because the same is safe and safety is essential. Resistance may have a loud voice at times, but it's not as loud as your desire for freedom, healing, and growth.

That's the truth. You embody polarities.

Which means both parts of you — the part that seeks safety and the part that longs for growth — are true, right, and worthy. They don't need to compete. They can work together, side by side, expanding your capacity, keeping you safe, and supporting your growth in a sustainable way.

Let's make some space, maybe with a deep breath, and allow this resistance to take shape: Perhaps as a dance partner.

Take a short journey with me into your imagination. Imagine stepping onto the dance floor, holding your own hand.

With each step forward, welcome any contraction, fear, or breath-holding that arises for you. Give it all space, as each one is a natural sensation. Breathe in as you welcome these parts of you; your whole self, and the whole of your expansion. The past, present, and future versions of you.

Feel what it's like to experience unconditional acceptance and love for every part of you. Notice how your body responds to each of these as you welcome them in. Notice how your body responds to welcoming *all* of who you are, and all of your experience, knowing that no piece of you needs to hide or pretend to be what it's not. You get to be all of it, and you get to hold your own hand while you do it.

This is a journey toward embodied wholeness.

You're on a journey toward seeing yourself as whole, and truly believing that there is nothing to fix about you because there is nothing that could ever be wrong about you. The idea of "wrongness" is a mental construct, one created by humans. Which means it doesn't exist on its own, and only holds the power that you give it.

There's a really notable yoga sutra that speaks to this truth. Sutra 4.15 in Swami Satchidananda's translation is my personal favorite. It says: *Vastu-sāmye citta-bhedāt tayor vibhaktah panthāh* — "The same object is perceived in different ways by different minds, leading to varying experiences of that object."

This sutra reminds us that reality is shaped by our perception. The idea of something being "wrong" or "right" doesn't exist inherently; it's not a fact or a universal truth.

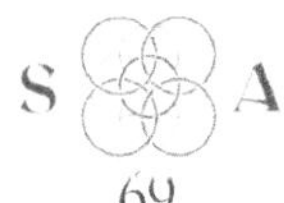

"Right" and "wrong" are constructs colored by the mind and by the stories we tell ourselves based on our lived experiences, or the experiences of our parents and loved ones.

Just as different people can experience the same situation in completely different ways, what you perceive as wrong or flawed in yourself is simply a reflection of your mind's perception – not an ultimate truth.

When you realize that these perceptions are constructs, you begin to dissolve the hold they have over you. Instead, you can step into a space of acceptance, seeing that you are already whole – already enough – exactly as you are now. And you are inherently worthy, as well.

With this in mind, it becomes clear that our personal narratives are just that: Stories we've written about ourselves, or that we've agreed to let others write about us.

Just as your perception can shift, so can your internal dialogue.

Wholeness reminds us that everything we could ever need is already inside of us, right now. It reminds us of how capable we are. How strong, how intuitive, how powerful and deserving we are... and then some.

There is also a part of you that feels afraid; afraid that if you grow, you might get hurt, or that change might hurt your relationships (and your relationships are *everything*).

This part of you is afraid to lose what you have in order to gain what you want.

This fear is real. It's real and it's valid, and it deserves to be honored. Can you honor it now with a deep breath? It's safe to hold this fear with care.

Growth can be scary, love. It's your mind's job to protect you from the unknown. Honoring and tending to this protective part of you is an act of self-love and self-compassion. You are becoming your own support system.

You can make peace with the fact that he (remember, the mind is masculine) is protecting you to the best of his ability. For him, that means keeping everything exactly the same. The masculine loves sameness. There is divine, god-like energy in sameness. However, the logical mind does not always account for how change could make you, your life, and your relationships *even better*. He prefers certainty, even if it's false.

You may often find yourself staying in relationships or jobs or even homes that are not aligned with your highest good. They might contradict what you desire most, but you stay because they are familiar. There is safety in what is known, and that's okay. It's safe to go at your own pace and to stay in consent with the tender parts of you that need more time. "Move at the speed of trust," says Kennae Miller, a dear teacher I met in Charleston.

As you journey through this process, new knowledge will emerge, inviting you to listen deeply. It will ask you to grow, expand, and reach for more, because you deserve more. You deserve all good.

It's okay for your desire to grow and your desire for safety to coexist. You can hold them both.

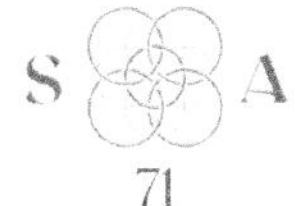

You get to be both and you get to feel both. Your ability to embrace the opposing forces within you is part of the alchemical process. This is a practice of nervous system regulation and self parenting; it expands your capacity to navigate life's inevitable changes while holding even more of what you desire most.

This is also an experience that is full of uncertainty. You're not going to know how to do it, and you're not meant to, because each experience is unique. Every day you wake up in this life, you are different. You have millions of new cells today that you didn't have yesterday.

This journey gets to look like you. It isn't about becoming more or fixing what's "broken." It's about remembering that you are already whole, just as you are.

When we embrace this truth, we stop searching outside ourselves for validation or completeness. It's a shift from tirelessly seeking and striving outward. Instead, we come home to ourselves, recognizing that the answers, peace, and love we seek have always been inside.

| Creating Safety

The thing your resistance may also not be aware of yet is that you create your own experience of safety. Growth can feel really unsafe because it's scary and unknown, and you don't know who you're going to be at the end of it – what edges you'll expand, what new space you'll grow into, and so on. But here's the beautiful truth: You are the one who decides what is safe. You also get to change your mind as many times as you would like to, as new information enters your awareness.

Maybe it's the truth that protects you.
Maybe it's joy that keeps you safe.

Either way, the power is yours. You get to decide; not your parents, not your teachers, not your partner, not society, and not your limiting beliefs about yourself and the world. You get to be responsible for your safety and you get to decide what works for you and what doesn't.

The one constant you will have on this journey is that everything will change. You can resist it or welcome it. When you learn how to be with your own internal conflict, you grow stronger. It's not about avoiding discomfort, but about being present with it, allowing yourself to hold space for the complexities within you. When you learn to sit with opposing forces – your fears, desires, doubts, and hopes – you'll discover that your presence has the power to alchemize them. The simple act of witnessing yourself, without judgment, will begin to transform the conflict within. This is an act of true liberation.

When you can hold space for the conflicts inside of you, external conflict will feel like a cake walk. Having a tough conversation or setting a boundary with someone is peanuts when you've already fought your own internal war and wrestled with your own shit.

The more you practice, the more resilient you become. Some teachers call this the "unfuckable" energy, because once you've grown accustomed to holding the intensity of your own emotions, no one else's can really get to you. This is a kind of self-mastery, of really *knowing* yourself.

Life will still bring challenges, but instead of being taken out by them, you'll feel a sense of steadiness and grace within yourself. You'll move through the world with a quiet, unshakable strength. Life won't feel so overwhelming because you've cultivated the capacity to hold your own truth, no matter what arises externally.

Nothing outside of you can take you away from yourself without your expressed permission. The decision is yours, you have sovereignty, and there is nothing you are not fully capable of handling.

With this new power of decision, I hope you'll decide to welcome life's grand dance.

When you do, you welcome your wholeness in.
When you do, you welcome your unique medicine.
When you do, you claim your innate intelligence.
When you do, you return to your soul home.

| Holding Opposites and Ambiguity

Humans naturally embody polarities. To better understand energetic influence, let's explore the difference between polarity and ambiguity.

Polarity is natural.

It exists everywhere in nature: Every poison has an antidote, and every antidote has a poison. Light is created by darkness, and darkness is created by the absence of light. We are not speaking in absolutes here; absolutes are mental constructs created from the desire for certainty. Instead, we are speaking about the nature of paradox and how it is a naturally occurring phenomenon. Which is why, when I invite you to welcome all aspects of yourself, even the ones that feel opposing, it is a natural experience of contrast.

Ambiguity is self-imposed confusion.

Google defines ambiguity as "the quality of being open to more than one interpretation" and includes synonyms like obscurity, enigma, vagueness, and uncertainty.

When we're having a conversation around self-responsibility and self-empowerment, I find ambiguity is an *intentional indecision* created to keep yourself in a victim mentality. In other words, ambiguity fuels martyrdom.

Personally, I've used ambiguity as a way to create the illusion of "having it all" while avoiding the risk of taking full responsibility.

Ambiguity allowed me to stay safely in the middle, and it gave me room to blame others when things went wrong. I could say things like, “Well, that wasn’t my idea. I just went along with it because I thought you knew what you were doing.”

Or, “I can’t believe you didn’t know this would happen. I’m upset with your choice to involve me.”

Does any of this sound familiar?

Ambiguity, when used this way, is the opposite of self-responsibility. By keeping the door open to blame others when things go awry, you completely negate your own power as a human being. You also relinquish your innate ability to influence your surroundings. Ambiguity, in this way, becomes a tool for disempowerment, leading to feelings of sadness, confusion, and being lost.

In contrast, holding opposites is a natural part of growth. You can hold where you are now and the goal you desire at the same time. Philosophers often hold “right” and “wrong” in the same conversation for deeper understanding because they know as soon as you label something, it limits that idea’s ability to change or evolve.

Once you recognize the emotional, energetic, and physical toll that ambiguity takes, you begin to understand the true power of decision. Deciding in favor of, and taking action to create the experience you want to have, will have a much greater impact on your mindbodyheart than nearly any other tool or technique you’ll find in this book. That's why I’m sharing it with you now.

Decisions denote self-respect, self-confidence, and self-honoring. They're also an advanced technique for energetic mastery. While decisions can feel vulnerable or shaky at first, they lead to clear and honest outcomes. They require and inspire maturity.

Immaturity, on the other hand, is wanting what you cannot have and savoring more in the *wanting* part of desire versus the *having* part.

Decisions teach you what you truly desire. As you become clearer about what you want, you gain clarity about the decisions required to make it happen. Maturity allows you to receive the results of your actions and to feel the contentment that comes with truly having what you desire.

Indecision is the obstacle to influence. Decision is the act of causing "the effect" that your life becomes; it is the act of shaping the life you wish to live.

| A Personal Note

I wrote this section after a sad, very sudden break-up when I was 34. I was dating a soulmate who held pain so deep, it made mine look like the edible glitter on Christmas cookies.

He was my soul's best friend. And he wasn't, all at the same time.

I didn't "recognize" him the moment we met, but when I did, it was like an awakening. I had been waiting for him for years — having visions of him in my early 20s, knowing he would walk into my life eventually.

When did meet, his soul was intact, but his life force, his energy, was a shadow of what it could be — a withered, hollow whisper of his true potential. His true self was merely an echo in his bones. He carried a flavor of fear inside his heart that most people never have the misfortune to meet.

What I recognized in him, and what drove me a little crazy, was that he lived his life in ambiguity. He wanted things and expressed them out loud, all while making high-level, intellectual excuses for why he couldn't have them and convincing himself they were out of reach. He acted like he wanted a beautiful life, but underneath, he was trapped in a relentless trauma loop that drained the very life from his crystal blue eyes.

Wanting wasn't safe for him; his childhood had taught him this harsh lesson.

His psychological foundation lacked the confidence to support a desire as good and beautiful as our relationship, and it crumbled under the weight of what he longed for but couldn't hold. He was frozen in place, using a fortress of logic to shield himself from the possibility of embracing the life he desired but couldn't trust, and I got hurt in the process.

Ultimately, I had to end the relationship. I had to get the closure I needed on my own and make peace with the fact that my soul's best friend, a man I will love for the rest of my existence, had manipulated me into believing he was someone he wasn't. He was lying to himself, not to me. But I still felt the pain for us both as I picked up the pieces of my heart and turned the lemons of this lesson into lemonade.

It's easy to want things: To get stuck in the wanting, and spend your life desiring something different but never taking the steps to have it. The drama of wanting can be addictive. It becomes a cycle, a comfortable space where you don't have to risk the vulnerability of actually going after what you desire. You stay in the story of "someday" because it's easier than facing the possibility of failure or loss. Wanting is easy. But *having*? That takes courage.

It takes courage to put yourself out there, to go after what you truly want, and risk the possibility that you might lose it. It takes guts to claim something for yourself and say, "This is mine." When you step out of wanting and into having, you face a whole new level of vulnerability — the fear that what you desire could slip through your fingers, or that it might not make you as happy as you thought it would.

And yet, there's real power in having. There's real power in stepping beyond the safety of desire and embracing the fullness of life. It's radical, actually, because once you do, you begin to live from a place of authenticity — and the unknown becomes your playground.

I say all this because true healing is hard work. True healing requires courage. True healing asks you to look at the things that cause you pain and suffering and hold them tenderly. It requires you to take responsibility for your own healing, even when it feels impossible.

Holding the broken pieces of your heart and creating something beautiful from them is warrior-level courage.

I discovered alchemy because I *had* to make something good out of the terrible things that had happened. I had to create meaning from the pain so that I could sleep at night, so I could dream of a better world where human beings care enough to do their inner work.

Because the best thing you can do for everyone in your life is take responsibility for your own healing. When you heal yourself, you heal everyone around you.

Embodiment + Ritual

Letting everything ground in and take root

| Embodiment + Integration

Embodiment and integration are the two most important pieces of this journey. Take your time with what's offered to you here.

You don't have to be in the depth of *non-stop* healing. Embodiment and rituals create a continuum; they hold you in the day-to-day while also grounding you in the long-term practice of being with yourself.

You are highly encouraged to make these rituals your own. Try them out and allow them to evolve in response to where you are and what you need in the moment. As my dear client and friend, Zen Jen, says: "I'm going to move today. Which kind of movement does my body want?"

Some days you may wish to spend the entire day in ritual. Other days, you might not get five minutes. Let it all be a part of your journey without judgment.

Embodiment is the process of becoming the living message of your soul's true essence. It has to happen over time, through repetition, daily inquiry, and tiny changes that feel really profound. It's how the feeling keeps going. It's how the awakening plants itself inside your consciousness, like a seed.

True enlightenment happens from the neck down, bridging knowledge from your brain to your body. It allows what you know to be *lived* and *felt* within you, slowly dissolving the lies you once believed. It's brave to be truly alive, living by your own set of rules and being guided by soul-level truths.

Living for yourself is a true rebellion.

Living with purpose is a force so strong, it offers permission to complete strangers.

Pay attention. The loving power of your true self can alchemize anything that meets you on your path. Whether you're transmuting pain, releasing falsehoods, or integrating your emotions and shadows, your embodied self will create the space for transformation.

You have the capacity to embody your divine nature as love itself. It's incredibly simple, in theory. And yet, our sweet, stubborn resistance will inevitably surface, making it challenging to practice.

As I mentioned earlier, the unconditional love and fire of devotion that exists in your heart and soul will automatically create alchemy. It is *inevitable.*

Once you know the truth, you can never experience a lie the same way again. That's what lasting change feels like — without the need to "make it hard."

Daily Ritual

Your soul is rooting for you

I invite you to meditate in three different ways each day for the next 30 days: Silent meditation, mantra (MAHN-trah) meditation, and moving meditation. You can practice all three together or sprinkle them throughout your day like nourishing snacks, or experiment with both. One meditation can be short and sweet, while another may long and drawn out. The choice is yours.

Remember, this practice is for you. There's no right or wrong way to approach it. Just show up and do what feels doable and supportive for where you are each day.

Trust yourself and let your intuition guide the way. You're building a relationship with yourself, and your soul is rooting for you. Follow what sets your heart ablaze.

The following ritual suggestions should take about 20 minutes, if you choose to do all three, for 6-7 minutes each.

1. Silent Meditation

Outer eyes close, and the inner eyes open.

I recommend meditating first thing in the morning, while in bed, before rising. Hit your snooze button and simply be with yourself for a few minutes. Tune into your desired outcome for the day ahead, offer yourself a full-body blessing, or practice your favorite silent meditation. Begin your day in quiet reverence, rooted in peace. Don't overcomplicated it.

My second favorite way to practice meditation is during the day, when you feel zapped and need 20-30 minutes of active rest. A siesta, so to speak. This is time to empty your brain of all the interactions you've had and become nothing. Let yourself dissolve into nothingness, becoming love itself.

For me, the most useful mediation practice is active rest without thought, or placing my hands on my body for self-healing. Actively share love with yourself, and open your mind to imagine what is possible.

2. Mantra Meditation

Let your voice carry you back to yourself.

Sound has the power to shift your energy and reconnect you with your center. Whether you whisper it quietly to yourself or sing it out loud, let mantra (MAHN-TRUH) be a tool to ground you into the present moment and cleanse your mental fields of heavy thought loops.

Sing along to your favorite mantras, or repeat them 108 times with a mala in hand. Let the sound of your voice and the repetition of the words anchor you in the present moment.

- For feeling connected to everything, use "**Om**", which is most powerful when sung, out loud, with a relaxed body.
- To access your truth and primal energy, chant "**So Ham**."
- For peace within the mind, chant "**Om Namah Shivaya**" (Oh-m Na-Mahh She-Vie-Yaa), which translates to, "I trust and act from the heart. I release what does not serve truth."

Put on mantra music and play it while you brush your teeth, singing along and letting the toothpaste drip out of your mouth. Why not? Life is messy and beautiful and fun.

Sing your mantra in the shower. Sing it in the car. Put it in your headphones so no one knows you're doing it.

You can even yell your mantra if you're having a particularly challenging day. Have fun with it and let it return you to your true self. If you have a mantra you already work with, feel free to stick with it or explore something new.

Pro Tip: This also works with your favorite song. Your brain cannot multitask, so when you sing, you're completely present. Try it!

3. Moving Meditation

Let your body move like a prayer.

Medicinal movement is an intuitive, embodied practice. Practice by putting on a piece of music that speaks to you (and your emotional state) and simply move your body in a way that feels nourishing.

If you're experiencing happiness, move to music that expands joy. If you're experiencing sadness, move to music that invites you to express and release sadness. For anger, choose high-energy music to help move the intensity through your system and reveal the softer underbelly beneath it. *Pro tip: Anger is often sadness in disguise.*

There is no right or wrong way to practice this meditation. Just move in a way that feels good, true, sacred, and holy.

Move like a prayer.
Move like nature.
Move like sunlight.
Move like deep grief.
Move like water.
Move like radiant love.

Let this movement be a reminder that you are your own medicine.

Conclusion

The sacred journey of healing

As we close the first book in the *Sacred Alchemy* series, I invite you to reflect on the depth of what you've uncovered within yourself. *What aspects have you been quietly nurturing within you?*

This book is more than a guide; hopefully it's a gentle hand, guiding you back to the alchemist within. Hopefully it's been a warm reminder of your power to heal in mind, body, and spirit, inviting you to reconnect with the deepest truths of your being and your potential.

I hope this experience has felt like a sacred, personal journey — a kind of energy healing occurring in each word you read. With every chapter, we've gotten to know each other better. We've peeled back the delicate layers of the inner landscape, making it feel more grounded and familiar. This journey has not been about a jolting, "burn it down" mentality, but rather a tender, loving dissolving of old patterns, creating space for new growth, clarity, and possibilities to emerge.

As you've moved through these teachings, you've been actively participating in your own healing, letting the practices and insights quietly infuse into your being. These intentional words are already working their subtle magic on the invisible currents of you.

I hope this journey has also given you a new language, a fresh lens through which to see your life and experiences. You now hold new keys, precious and powerful, to unlock the doors that once stood in your way. These are keys of inherent wisdom, showing you pathways that were always within you, silently whispering to be discovered.

These are the tools that will continue to open doors in your healing process and help you reveal new levels of insight, compassion, and authenticity. You can always return to them.

Remember, healing is an unfinished process. It is not meant to be viewed linearly as an accomplishment or destination. Instead, healing is a lifelong relationship with the deepest layers of your being, one that ripens and deepens with each revelation and each pause for self-reflection. And because there's no rush to the finish line, we get to honor each step as sacred.

Let everything you've learned here continue to settle into your being like seeds planted in rich soil, allowing time for them to root, grow, and blossom. Trust in the process and trust the pace of your integration. Be tender with yourself as the layers continue to unravel. Healing, like life itself, is a dance of patience, love, and grace, and you are exactly where you need to be in this moment.

Move forward knowing that this is only the beginning. There is always a deeper layer to explore, more light to uncover, and more magic to be revealed.

I invite you to continue this work with me in the next book, *Sacred Structure*, where we explore the foundations that hold and ground you. We delve into the root chakra and your relationship with what stabilizes you — your body, your home, your beliefs, and your connection to the Earth. This is the work of creating strong, supportive structures that sustain your growth and nurture your sense of belonging in the world.

Until we meet again, may the energy of this healing stay with you, reminding you that you are your own greatest healer and that everything you seek is already within you.

With love and reverence,

The Energy Cleansing Guidebook

Practical tools for clearing your energy field
+ keeping your energy sacred

| A Glimpse Inside My New E-Book

Imagine for a moment: The air is still, and your body is heavy with the weight of the day. It's not just a physical heaviness. Something deeper tugs at your spirit, leaving you feeling clouded and disconnected. That's the subtle pull of energy – energy that doesn't belong to you, but has found its way into your space.

When you take a moment to cleanse your energy, it's like stepping into a clear, flowing stream. You feel the weight lift, the fog clear, and your entire being realigns. Cleansing your energetic field is like returning home to yourself.

Taking responsibility for your energy is as essential as caring for your physical body. Just like you shower to cleanse your skin, your energy also needs regular clearing to stay balanced and healthy.

Throughout the day, your energy is constantly interacting with other people, places, and things.

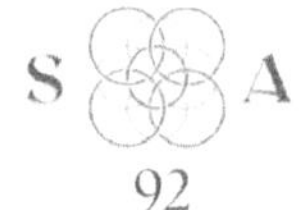

Whether it's a brief conversation, a challenging encounter, or even a quick scroll through social media, your energy is absorbing and exchanging vibrations. By cleansing regularly, you allow yourself to reset, just like stepping into a warm bath after a long day. It melts away the stress, restoring balance to your mind, body, and spirit.

Our energy can be impacted in many ways:

- Physical or emotional blocks
- A lack of social support
- Disconnection from self, nature, or spirit

Each day, you come into contact with the energetic fields of people, animals, the Earth, and more. This invisible exchange can profoundly affect your auric field. Have you ever received a text that tied your stomach in knots? Or visited a place where you felt instantly at peace? These are examples of aura impact. Negative encounters, like being yelled at by a stranger, can disrupt your energy and leave you feeling unsettled.

When I feel overwhelmed for no clear reason, I know my aura has been impacted. In these moments, I turn to an aura cleansing tool — like a salt bath, burning wand, or meditation — to regain balance and clarity.

If you teach, coach, offer therapy, or care for others, cleansing your auric field is essential. By maintaining your energy, you also uplift those you interact with. Remember: Your feelings are messages from your body, and many of these energy imbalances can be cleared within minutes.

| Ways to cleanse the energetic field

Water

Water is a natural conductor of energy and one of the most effective ways to cleanse your energetic field. Imagine water flowing over your body, carrying away any heaviness or tension you've absorbed throughout the day.

- How to use it: Simply wash your hands or take a bath with the intention of clearing your energy. Picture the water not only cleaning your skin but also your aura. If you can, spend time in a natural body of water like a lake, river, or the ocean for an even more powerful effect.

Salt

Salt is a natural purifier, used for centuries in spiritual practices for protection and cleansing. It helps neutralize negative energy and restore balance to your field.

- How to use it: Take a salt bath using sea salt or Himalayan salt to soak your body and clear your energy field. If a full bath isn't possible, try a salt scrub in the shower or keep a bowl of salt by your sink for a quick hand-cleansing ritual.

Aromatherapy

Essential oils carry the potent essence of plants, which vibrate at a high frequency and can shift your energy instantly. The power of scent connects deeply to the nervous system and can ground, soothe, or uplift your energy depending on the oil you choose.

- How to use: Rub a few drops of essential oil like lavender, sage, or rosemary on your palms and take a deep breath, inhaling the aroma. You can also diffuse essential oils in your space or wear them on your skin to keep your energy clear throughout the day.

Sound

Sound is a powerful healer, able to instantly shift your energy through vibration. Whether through music, chanting, or simply humming, sound brings you back into the present moment, allowing you to clear and align your field.

- How to use it: Sing, hum, or chant to create vibrations that move through your energy field. You can also listen to high-frequency music or sound baths to help cleanse and restore your energy.

Meditation

Meditation is one of the most direct ways to clear your energy. By sitting still and becoming aware of your thoughts and energy field, you can begin to release what no longer serves you.

- How to use it: Close your eyes, take a few deep breaths, and visualize your energy field being cleansed. You can imagine a beam of light entering your body, sweeping away any stuck or stagnant energy.

- *Pro Tip: If you're feeling scattered or overwhelmed, take five minutes to meditate. Visualize yourself skimming your energy field, like skimming a pool, to clear out any energetic debris.*

Burning Wands

Using a burning wand made of sage, palo santo, or copal is an ancient practice for clearing space and energy fields. The smoke from these plants helps cleanse and purify the energy around you.

- How to use it: Light your wand and wave the smoke around your body, starting from your feet and moving up towards your head. As you do this, set the intention for the smoke to clear any negative or stagnant energy from your field.

- *Pro Tip: Use a burning wand to cleanse not just your body, but also your space. Move the smoke through the rooms of your home to clear the energy of the environment as well.*

Intention

Your intention is one of the most powerful tools you have. You can shift the energy in your body and field on a cellular level simply by setting a clear intention.

- How to use it: When you set an intention, it's like creating a blueprint for your energy to follow. Take a moment to clarify what you want to release and what you want to invite in. A simple mantra you can use is: "Anything that is not mine, not meant for me, or not sourced in unconditional love, please leave my body, mind, spirit, and energetic fields. Thank you. You do not have my permission to be here. I now also release ________________."

- *Pro Tip: Set intentions not only for yourself but for your space and relationships. Create energetic boundaries by visualizing a field of protection around you that supports your well-being.*

Crystals

Crystals hold unique vibrations that can help clear, balance, and protect your energy field. Specific crystals like selenite, black tourmaline, and clear quartz are known for their cleansing and protective properties.

- How to use it: Hold a crystal in your hand or place it on your body while meditating. You can also keep crystals in your environment, like on your desk or by your bedside, to keep your energy clear and protected.

Mantra

Mantras are powerful words or phrases that, when spoken aloud, have the ability to manipulate energy. The sound vibrations created by mantras can cleanse your field and uplift your consciousness.

- How to use it: Chant mantras like "Om" to feel connected to everything around you, or "So Ham" to access deeper truth. Repeating mantras aloud aligns your energy with higher frequencies, and the repetition can help dissolve negative thought patterns.

Energy Healing

Sometimes, energy cleansing requires a deeper touch, and that's where energy healing comes in. Whether you seek out a healer (like myself!) or practice self-healing, energy work allows you to clear deeply held blocks in your field.

- How to use it: During an energy healing session, focus on relaxing and allowing the energy to flow through your body. This helps release emotional and energetic blockages, bringing harmony back to your system. Energy healing can leave you feeling vibrant, clear, and deeply at peace.

- *Pro Tip: Incorporate energy healing into your routine, especially after challenging times.* ***You can scan this QR code to learn more and book a remote session with me:***

Deservability Treatment

The Deservability Treatment is a type of energy healing that focuses on shifting your internal beliefs about what you deserve. It helps you clear away limitations and affirm that you are worthy of love, abundance, and good health.

- How to use it: Take a moment to sit in a quiet space, and read or recite words of affirmation such as: "I deserve all good. I release any limiting beliefs about myself and open up to the infinite possibilities before me." This treatment reprograms your energy field and helps you release self-imposed limitations.

- *Pro Tip: Record your Deservability Treatment in your own voice and listen to it daily. This will continuously shift your energy field to align with the belief that you are deserving of everything good.*

These are just a few of the many tools you can use to cleanse your energy. Choose the ones that resonate with you, and make them a regular part of your practice. Remember, the more often you cleanse your energy, the lighter and more aligned you'll feel.

Deservability Treatment

An excerpt from Louise Hay's *You Can Heal Your Life*

I am deserving. I deserve all good. Not some, not a little bit, but all good.

I now move past all negative, restricting thoughts. I release and let go of the limitations of my parents; I love them, and I go beyond them. I am not their negative opinions, nor their limiting beliefs. I am not bound by any of the fears or prejudices of the current society I live in. I no longer identify with limitations of any kind.

In my mind, I have total freedom. I now move into a new space of consciousness, where I am willing to see myself differently. I am willing to create new thoughts about myself and about my life. My new thinking becomes new experiences. I now know and affirm that I am at one with the Prospering Power of the Universe. As such, I now prosper in a number of ways.

The totality of possibilities lies before me. I deserve life, a good life. I deserve love, and abundance of love. I deserve good health. I deserve to live comfortably and to prosper. I deserve joy and happiness. I deserve freedom to be all that I can be. I deserve more than that. I deserve all good.

The Universe is more than willing to manifest my new beliefs. And I accept this abundant life with joy, pleasure, and gratitude. For I am deserving. I accept it, and I know it to be true.

Using The Energy Cleansing Guide

Imagine a life where you feel deeply grounded. Your energy is clear, and your personal space is protected — every single day.

The Energy Cleansing Guide is your companion on this journey, offering step-by-step practices to help you clear, balance, and maintain your energetic field.

Whether you're looking for simple daily practices or deeper, advanced rituals, this guide empowers you to release stagnant energy and protect yourself from unwanted influences. It's not just about clearing what doesn't serve you — it's about creating a sacred space within and around you, where your energy is vibrant, peaceful, and aligned with your true self.

In The Energy Cleansing Guide, we also explore energy healing and how energies manifest in the physical body, giving you tools to integrate energy work into your daily life. You'll learn how to create your own personal rituals, use a customizable ritual template for daily use, and deepen your trust in your intuition. You'll also explore connecting with your guides, aligning your energy with the flow of life, and much more.

This guide is perfect for empaths, healers, and anyone who interacts deeply with the world.

To get the guide, scan the QR code: 

What's Next?

How to go deeper and stay in the work.

This is the first book in the *Sacred Alchemy* series, a collection of work designed to help you heal your life through healing your body.

This book can be read in tandem with the Energetic Influence workbook where you'll find resources, practices, and tools to support you in exploring your practice further.

The Energetic Influence workbook invites you to:

- Check in and set intentions for each lesson's focus
- Practice embodiment and explore new ways of listening inwardly
- Witness your growth through compassionate reflection
- See what has shifted for you and where you specifically desire to focus your energy now
- Answer questions that dig deep and help you create a safe relationship with yourself/your body

The next book in this series is *Sacred Alchemy Book 2: Sacred Structure.*

Acknowledgements

Thank you is my favorite part.

Thank you to the sacred lands of Bacalar, Mexico. This land has held me in beautiful and profound ways and taught me more than any teacher I've ever met. Living here has helped me to get clear enough in my mindbodyheart to write, re-organize, edit, and complete this book with fierce integrity. I just don't think I could have written it anywhere else in the world.

Thank you to the women who made this book possible: Casey Higgins-Johnson and Rebecca Schonebaum. Thank you for your perseverance, devotion, and belief in me and this work.

Thank you to my father who knew I would create great things and never let me settle for anything less. Thank you for helping me to open the door to my gifts and hear my soul's calling.

Thank you to my mother, who has enthusiastically said yes to every crazy idea I've ever had because she knew I could make it happen.

- *Mom, I want to host my first retreat ever in Mexico.* "Yes, honey!"
- *Mom, I want to write eight books instead of one.* "Do it!"
- *Mom, I want to attend a month-long yoga teacher training in Costa Rica but I don't have any money.* "You should, I'll give you the loan."

Mom, thank you for always believing in me, and even more so, for giving me the means and the foundations to make my dreams come true.

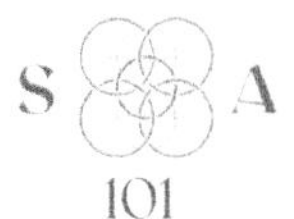

Thank you to my entire family for cheering me on! Thank you Landon, Jamie, and Laura. Thank you to my angel dog, Luna, who quite literally sat beside me while I brought this book together, and to my newest addition, Pimí, who now sits on my other side.

Thank you to my soul family: Hillary Sabbato, Casey Higgins-Johnson, and Stephanie Burg for standing beside me with fierce and unconditional love during the entire writing process. Thank you, Hillary, for your countless hours of transcriptions and for teaching me so much about sisterhood. Thank you, Casey, for holding me steady and for teaching me so much about partnership. Thank you, Stephanie, for your mentorship and multidimensional friendship, for your sacred devotion to your work, and for teaching me beyond words. Thank you for holding me in the depths of both joy and despair, and reminding me of what's possible when I trust in spirit.

Thank you to the founding members of the Sacred Alchemy Course: Emily, Casey, Hillary, Bob, Mandy, Courtney, Amelia, Katie, Gabby, Deborah, Stacy, Ashley, Laura, Candice, Mary, and Cory. Thank you for helping me bring this information to life and for being a part of this union in my work. There are no coincidences, and if I had not originally had you all to teach, I may still be procrastinating, today.

Thank you to the extraordinary teachers I have been gifted with in this lifetime: Dr. John Upledger, Stan the Man, Patrick O'Leary, Jessica Durivage, Sharon Gannon, David Life, Jeffrey Cohen, Rafael Cervantes, Andrea Boyd, Brian Hoke, Abigail McClam, Bill Bauerly, Nicole Rager, Stephanie Burg, Jessica Rueger, Wendy Taylor, LuLi Labat, Zara Trejo, Valeria Bruschini, Dori Chitayat, Hunab Amaya, and my first spiritual teacher, my mother, Missy Sunshine.

Thank you to little LuLu. You are fierce as fuck, girl. If writing this series has taught me anything, it's that I can persevere. My grandmother used to wear a heart-shaped amulet with a mustard seed inside and a bible verse on the back. It said, roughly: "If you have faith the size of a mustard seed, you can move mountains." I was obsessed with it. The necklace, the message, and my grandmother's wearing of it because I knew she believed it and that meant I could believe it, too. I also knew (and she knew) that *nothing* was ever going to stop me.

I want to thank God. Thank you, Great Spirit. Thank you for the protective, all-loving, and divine energies you have surrounded me with during this process. Thank you for letting me project my anger, rage, and kaleidoscope of emotions onto you, and for still loving me. Thank you for always bringing me back home and reminding me of what's most important. Thank you.

And lastly, I want to thank you, reader. Without you, books don't exist. Without students, teachers don't exist. Without someone to share with, we are never able to fully express and realize our visions.

You make it all possible. I love you.

Made in the USA
Middletown, DE
21 January 2025